Cybersecurity

Unlock Your Potential, The Beginner's Guide to a Rewarding Career

A Practical Guide for
Hispanics/Latinos and All Our Allies

Eric J. Belardo

TABLE OF CONTENTS

DEDICATION

Dedicated to my Wife, Carmen

You are my reason to keep going every day!

I also want to dedicate this book to The Next generation of Cyber Defenders. You are our future!

Unidos Se Puede!

Together We Can!

PREFACE

"I want to learn cyber."

I've heard this phrase thousands of times in my 30+ year career: *"I want to learn cyber."* My response is always the same: "That's like saying, 'I want to learn healthcare.' Doesn't sound right, does it? We have doctors, nurses, X-ray techs, phlebotomists, educators, office managers, and many more trades that make healthcare work. In the field of cyber, we have **over 50 different trades** supporting the operations that keep us secure from cybercrime. There are roles like security operation center (SOC) analysts, vulnerability analysts, security architects, forensics analysts, and more. So, what specific area of cybersecurity do you want to learn about?"

The next thing I always hear is, *"But I want to learn how to hack."* I get it. Hacking is the most visible part of cybersecurity in popular culture. But it's not usually the easiest way to get into the field. That's because the area requires a lot of education, experience, and time. And let's be realistic: there are only a few entry-level hacking jobs.

But people need to realize you have to learn how cybercriminals attack us so that we can learn how to defend against them. So, even if you're not starting as a "hacker" yourself, you will still obtain the basic skills of offensive operations in cybersecurity. In other words, don't feel like you have to be a hacker to get into cybersecurity. There are a variety of roles in the field, and most of them require at least a basic understanding of how cyberattacks work.

Cybersecurity is a vast field with many different specialties. It's essential to narrow down your interests **before** starting your learning journey so you can focus on the skills and knowledge most relevant to your career goals.

"I've heard that I must be a math and science expert and know how to code/program to be in cybersecurity."

Cybersecurity careers and trades **are not** just for math and science wizards!

There are many cybersecurity roles, and some require different knowledge and skills. For example, security analysts need to understand and analyze complex technical information, but they don't need to be able to code (it helps with automating, but it's not a requirement). Incident responders need to be able to think critically and troubleshoot problems quickly, but they don't need to be math experts.

Even roles that do require some coding skills, such as penetration testers and security engineers, don't need a deep understanding of math or science. Many resources are available to help people learn to code without a strong background in these subjects.

In addition to technical skills, many cybersecurity jobs require strong communication, problem-solving, and teamwork skills. So, if you're interested in a career in cybersecurity, don't let the idea that you need to be a math and science expert or know how to code stop you. There's sure to be a cybersecurity job that fits your skills and interests well.

As I mentioned earlier, I've been working in the field for over three decades, and I take immense pride in my Puerto Rican Hispanic/Latino heritage. Helping others find the thrill and passion in this ever-evolving field is personally exciting and rewarding for me.

I've worn many hats throughout my journey, working on various projects with government, commercial and international companies. I've even had the privilege of leading teams in cutting-edge areas. On top of that, I've been lucky to travel to and work in more than 25 countries across the globe. It's been a fantastic adventure, and I'm eager to share that excitement with others.

Over the years, I began to notice something quite upsetting - the lack of representation of Hispanics/Latinos in the field of cybersecurity.

In 2021, a few individuals approached me with the same observation, and my response was straightforward: "You're right. For the first 20 years of my career, I often found myself as the sole Hispanic/Latino in many of those jobs and meeting rooms." It was crystal clear that we needed to take action.

"The Birth of Raices Cyber Org"

As I mentioned, in the summer of 2021, a few cybersecurity friends came to me with a concern. They had just attended several conferences and noticed very few Hispanics there. They wanted to do something about it.

Given my 33 years in the field, I wasn't surprised, but their concern got me thinking. I contacted my dear friend, Dr. Aunshul Rege, who leads the Temple University Cybersecurity in Application, Research, and Education (CARE) Lab. I asked her and her team to research whether a cybersecurity group existed to help Hispanics and Latinos.

She came back to me with the answer: **zero**. Sure, there were other Hispanic/Latino organizations with subgroups or rooms focused on helping people in cybersecurity, but no organizations were solely focused on helping our community thrive.

I've never considered myself a "social justice warrior, " and I wasn't interested in this topic. My focus has always been to keep my head down and do my best for my career. But this time, something within me said: **"You have to do this."** I locked myself in a room for a week and thought about it long and hard. (More on this in Chapter 5).

By the end of the week, I had a plan. **I created Raices Cyber Org**.

Raices Cyber Org's mission is to empower, encourage, and support Hispanic, Latino, Latina, and Latinx individuals to achieve greater representation in the cyber workforce through education, mentorship, and advocacy. We provide access to resources, training, and mentorship and raise awareness about the importance of cybersecurity in the modern digital world.

(Website: https://raicescyber.org LinkedIn: https://www.linkedin.com/company/raicescyberorg)

We work with community partners to create a safer and more secure digital environment for all Hispanic, Latino, Latina, and Latinx individuals and communities, focusing on underserved populations.

Our ultimate goal is to build a more resilient and inclusive cybersecurity workforce and digital society free from discrimination and inequality.

In the past few years, we've grown into an international community with over 17+ city support groups in the continental United States and over three support groups outside the US in Canada, the Dominican Republic, and Puerto Rico. At the time of writing this book, our membership was over 4700 people. In October 2023, we held our first in-person conference and summit, with nearly 300 attendees. (https://raicescon.org).

By purchasing this book, you're supporting the mission of Raices Cyber Org. A portion of the proceeds from this book will go directly to support our mission of bringing more Hispanics and Latinos into the field of cybersecurity.

Thank you for your support!

After many years of helping thousands of people get into cybersecurity, I decided to write this book to help you understand the field of cybersecurity and how to get started.

"What will you discover in these pages?"

As I said before, I wrote this book after many years of helping thousands of people get into cybersecurity to help you understand how to start your journey in the field. Cybersecurity is a broad field that covers everything from protecting computer systems from hackers to keeping your personal information safe online. It's a challenging but gratifying career path, and there's a lot of demand for skilled cybersecurity professionals.

This book is a guide that will introduce you to the basics of cybersecurity, from the different types of cyberattacks that cybersecurity professionals have to defend against. You'll also learn about the different career paths available in cybersecurity and how to develop the skills and knowledge you need to be successful. Along the way, I will also give you some helpful tips on finding a great job in cybersecurity and continuing to succeed in the field. The following are some topics we cover in this book:

- What is cybersecurity, and why is it important?

- The different types of cyberattacks

- The different career paths available in cybersecurity

- The challenges for our Hispanic/Latino/Latina/Latinx community and how to address these

- How do you develop the power skills and knowledge you need to be successful in cybersecurity

- Tips on how to find a great job in cybersecurity and how to continue to succeed in the field

So, if you're interested in learning about careers in cybersecurity from someone who has been where you are, **this book is for you.** I'll walk you through everything you need to know to get started and succeed.

"Unidos Se Puede / United We Can"

INTRODUCTION

What is Cybersecurity?

I have always defined Cybersecurity as the art and science of protecting computer systems, networks, and digital data from various forms of unauthorized access, damage, or theft. It encompasses multiple strategies and technologies to safeguard information and ensure digital assets' confidentiality, integrity, and availability. Cybersecurity has become a critical concern in an increasingly interconnected world, where information and communication technologies are integral to daily life and business operations.

Cybersecurity is an art because it also requires creativity, intuition, and problem-solving skills. Cybersecurity professionals must be able to think creatively, have diverse thoughts, and develop new and innovative ways to protect against cyber threats. They must also understand the attackers' motivations and anticipate their next moves.

Why is cybersecurity critical to our modern lives?

In this increasingly interconnected world, Cybersecurity is crucial because it protects our computers, networks, and data from being attacked and our information stolen or made unavailable. This includes personal information like our names, addresses, Social Security numbers, and credit card numbers, as well as financial data like our bank account numbers and investment information. It also includes intellectual property like trade secrets and proprietary information.

Cyber attacks can be costly and damaging, both financially and reputationally. For example, a data breach can cost a company millions of dollars in remediation costs and lost revenue. A ransomware attack can shut down a company's operations until the company pays the ransom. Denial-of-service attacks can make a company's website or online services unavailable to customers. The cost of recovering from these can bankrupt small companies and cost millions for larger organizations. In addition to these costs, the company's reputation can suffer, leading to loss of customers.

Cybersecurity is also essential for individuals. We rely on computers and networks to communicate, bank, shop, and access government services. Cyber attacks can steal our personal information, lead to financial losses, and even damage physical infrastructure.

Here are some real examples of the importance of cybersecurity for individuals:

- **It protects our personal information:** Cyber attacks can steal personal information, such as names, addresses, Social Security numbers, and credit card numbers. With this information, criminals can commit identity theft, fraud, and other crimes.

- **It protects our financial data:** Cyber attacks can steal financial data like bank account numbers and investment information. Cybercriminals can steal money from victims' accounts and make unauthorized purchases.

- **It Protects our intellectual property:** Cyber attacks can steal intellectual property, such as trade secrets and proprietary information. This can give competitors an unfair advantage and damage a company's bottom line.

- **It Protects our critical infrastructure:** Cyber attacks can target critical infrastructure, such as power grids, transportation systems, and water treatment facilities. This can disrupt essential services and have a significant impact on public safety.

Cybersecurity is an essential issue for everyone, and you must take steps to protect yourself from cyber-attacks. By following cybersecurity best practices, you can help to reduce your risk of becoming a victim of a cyber attack.

Why is it essential for Hispanics & Latinos to be involved in cybersecurity?

First, Latinos are increasingly targeted by cybercriminals. According to a 2022 report by the Anti-Defamation League, Latinos are more likely than the general population to be victims of online scams. The report found that **14% of Latinos have been victims of online scams**, compared to 11% of the general population. A 2021 report by the Federal Trade Commission found that Latinos are more likely than the general population to report losing money to fraud. The report found that **40% of Latinos who reported fraud lost money**, compared to 30% of the general population. A 2020 report by the National Cybersecurity Alliance found that Latinos are more likely than the general population to be victims of identity theft. The report found that **18% of Latinos have been victims of identity theft**, compared to 13% of the general population.

These startling statistics are likely due to several factors, including the fact that Latinos are more likely to use prepaid debit cards and other forms of payment that are easier for cybercriminals to steal from. Additionally, Latinos are more likely to speak Spanish, which makes them easier for Spanish-speaking cybercriminals to target.

Second, Latinos are underrepresented in the cybersecurity workforce. According to 2021 reports, the number of Hispanics/Latinos in the cyber workforce is between 4% to 5%. This lack of representation is a problem because fewer cybersecurity professionals understand the unique needs and challenges of the Latino community.

Third, Latinos have a lot to offer in the cybersecurity field. Latinos are diverse people with a wide range of skills and experiences. Additionally, Latinos are often bilingual and bicultural, giving them a unique perspective that can be invaluable in cybersecurity.

Here are some specific ways that Hispanics & Latinos can get involved in cybersecurity:

- **Pursue a career in cybersecurity.** There are many different career paths in cybersecurity, including security analysts, network engineers, and ethical hackers. Several organizations offer training and certification programs in cybersecurity.

- **Volunteer your time to help others learn about cybersecurity.** Many organizations need volunteers to help teach others about cybersecurity. You can volunteer to teach classes, give presentations, or write blog posts.

- **Advocate for cybersecurity awareness in the Latino community.** You can advocate for cybersecurity awareness in the Latino community by talking to your family and friends about cybersecurity, sharing cybersecurity tips on social media, and attending cybersecurity events.

By getting involved in cybersecurity, Hispanics/Latinos can help to protect themselves and their community from cybercrime. Additionally, Latinos can help to make the cybersecurity field more diverse and inclusive.

How can we all make the field of Cybersecurity more welcoming to Hispanics & Latinos?

For those already in the cybersecurity field, one way to make the cybersecurity field more welcoming to Latinos is to create mentorship and sponsorship programs. These programs can help Latinos learn from experienced professionals and build their networks. Latinos need to become more visible as we all want to see ourselves represented where we want to go.

Another way to make cybersecurity more accessible to Latinos is to make training and certification programs more affordable by offering scholarships, Financial assistance, and programs in Spanish.

Finally, we can promote cybersecurity awareness in the Latino community by partnering with Latino community organizations and creating cybersecurity resources in Spanish.

By taking these steps, we can create a more inclusive cybersecurity field where everyone has the opportunity to succeed and reach more Hispanics & Latinos.

Here are some tangible ideas we should all consider and advocate for

- A cybersecurity company could partner with a local Latino community organization to create a mentorship program for Latino students interested in cybersecurity.

- A cybersecurity training company could offer scholarships to Latinos who want to take their courses or provide student scholarships to Latino Organizations.

- Cybersecurity conferences could offer Spanish-language sessions and workshops and market to the Hispanic/Latino market.

By taking these steps, we can make the cybersecurity field more welcoming and accessible to Hispanics and Latinos and grow our representation.

How should you use this book?

This book guides Hispanics/Latinos and all our allies who are interested in learning more about cybersecurity and pursuing a career in the field. You can use it in several ways depending on your needs and goals.

If you are new to cybersecurity, read the book's first few chapters for a general overview. These chapters cover the basics of cybersecurity, such as what it is, why it is essential, and the different types of cyber threats.

Once you have a basic understanding of cybersecurity, you can explore the different career paths available. The book includes chapters on various cybersecurity jobs, such as security analyst, network engineer, and ethical hacker. Each chapter provides information about the job duties, skills, and education and training required for each position.

If you are already interested in a specific cybersecurity career path, you can use the book to learn more about the skills and education you need to be successful. Each chapter in a particular cybersecurity job includes a section on skills and education required. This section provides information on the specific skills and knowledge employers seek and the different educational programs and certifications that can help you develop these skills and knowledge.

The book also includes several resources for Latinos interested in cybersecurity or finding a job. These resources include links to cybersecurity organizations, websites, and job boards.

Here are some additional tips for using this book:

- Use the book as a reference guide. You don't have to read it from cover to cover. Feel free to skip to the chapters most relevant to your needs and interests.

- **Highlight important passages and take notes**. This will help you remember the information that you have read.

- Use the resources mentioned in each chapter to learn more about the topics covered in the chapter.

If you have any questions, please contact us in Raices Cyber Org (https://raicescyber.org | https://www.linkedin.com/company/raicescyberorg) for help. Many people are willing to help Latinos and other underrepresented groups succeed in cybersecurity.

This book will become a valuable resource for you as you start your journey into cybersecurity.

Eric J. Belardo, NSA IAM, CEIM, CFI&I

"The Cyber Papa"

Founder & Executive Director

Raices Cyber Org

CHAPTER 1

The Basics of Cybersecurity

What are the different types of cyber threats?

What is a **cyber threat**? A cyber threat is a potential troublemaker lurking in the digital shadows. It can mess with your computer systems, networks, or digital stuff. These threats come from many sneaky folks with bad intentions, like hackers, cybercriminals, or even nation-states. They use tactics like hacking, spreading malware, tricking people with phishing emails, or crashing websites. Their goal? To exploit weaknesses and cause chaos, steal information, or make a mess of things in the digital world. Cybersecurity professionals work hard to spot and stop these threats so our digital lives can stay safe and sound. The following are just a few examples of potential cyber threats, but many other threats could occur:

- **Malware** is malicious software that can damage or disable your computer system. Malware spreads through email attachments, infected websites, or USB drives. Common types of malware include viruses, trojans, and worms.

- **Phishing attacks** are emails or websites that trick you into revealing personal information, such as your passwords or credit card numbers. Phishing attacks often look like they are from a legitimate company, such as your bank or credit card company.

- **Social engineering attacks** trick you into performing actions that compromise security to reveal information that can be used maliciously. Social engineering attacks can be done via phone, in person, or online. Common social engineering attacks include phishing and vishing.

- **Denial-of-service attacks** are attempts to overwhelm a website or server with traffic so legitimate users cannot access it.

In addition to these general cyber threats, several specific threats can target businesses and organizations. These cyber-threats can include:

- **Advanced persistent threats (APTs):** APTs are highly sophisticated cyber attacks designed to steal sensitive data or disrupt operations. APTs are generally executed by nation-state actors or organized crime syndicates.

- **Ransomware:** Ransomware is a type of malware that encrypts your data and demands a ransom payment in exchange for the decryption key. Ransomware attacks can be very costly and disruptive for businesses and organizations.

- **Supply chain attacks:** Supply chain attacks target the suppliers of a business to gain access to the business or organization's systems or data. Supply chain attacks can be challenging to detect and prevent.

These are just a few of the many types of cyber threats. New cyber threats are constantly being developed and discovered, so it is vital to stay informed about the latest threats and to take steps to protect yourself and your organization from cyber-attacks.

Why do cybercriminals do what they do?

Cybercriminals attack people and organizations for various reasons; most are driven by personal gain, ideology, or malicious intent. The following are some of the motivations behind these cybercriminal activities.

- **Financial Gain:** Many cybercriminals are motivated by money. They may seek to steal sensitive financial information, commit fraud, engage in identity theft, or demand money through activities like ransomware attacks. Cybercrime can be lucrative, and the profit potential is a significant driver.

- **Data Theft:** Cybercriminals may target valuable data such as personal information, credit card numbers, intellectual property, or trade secrets. This stolen data is sold on the dark web or used maliciously.

- **Hacktivism:** Some individuals or groups engage in cyberattacks as protest or activism. They may target government websites, corporations, or other entities to advance a political or social cause.

- **Espionage:** Nation-states and intelligence agencies may conduct cyber espionage to gather intelligence, monitor rival nations, or steal sensitive government or corporate data.

- **Vandalism and Disruption:** Some cybercriminals aim to disrupt online services, deface websites, or create chaos for no apparent personal gain. These attacks may be carried out for bragging rights or to promote an ideological message.

- **Blackmail and Extortion:** Cybercriminals may threaten to release sensitive information or launch further attacks unless a victim pays a ransom or complies with their demands.

Extortion is common in cases of data breaches or ransomware attacks.

- **Competitive Advantage:** Some businesses and individuals engage in cyberattacks to gain a competitive advantage. This may involve stealing intellectual property, customer lists, or trade secrets from competitors.

- **Revenge:** Individuals with personal vendettas may sometimes launch cyberattacks against specific targets to seek revenge or damage their reputation.

- **Testing and Experimentation:** Some cybercriminals use hacking and attacks to test their skills, discover vulnerabilities, or experiment with new techniques. These activities may lead to future, more sophisticated attacks.

- **Thrill-Seeking:** A small portion of cybercriminals engage in illegal activities purely for the thrill and challenge of it. Hacking can be addictive for some individuals.

- **State-Sponsored Cyber Warfare:** Nation-states may use cyberattacks to undermine other countries' infrastructure, gather intelligence, or conduct offensive military operations.

Understanding the reasons and motivations of cybercriminals is essential for developing effective cybersecurity strategies and protective measures.

As the cyber threat landscape evolves, individuals and organizations must stay vigilant and proactive in defending against these diverse and ever-changing threats.

How can you protect yourself and your family from cyber-attacks? Basic cybersecurity best practices

Let's discuss how to keep yourself and your family safe from cyberattacks in your everyday life:

- **Use Strong Passwords:** Think of creating strong, unique passwords like crafting a secret code. Use a mix of capital and small letters, numbers, and symbols. Avoid easy-to-guess stuff like birthdays or common words. And if you've got too many to remember, consider using a password manager to help you.

- **Enable 2FA/ MFA (Multi-Factor Authentication)** - "The Extra Lock." Imagine having a second lock on your front door. Two-factor authentication (2FA) is like that for your online accounts. It adds an extra layer of protection by asking for a code sent to your phone or using a second authenticator app when you log in.

- **Keep Everything Updated:** *(Patch your Stuff)* You know how you get those updates on your phone or computer? They're like bug fixes for your software. Always make sure your stuff is up-to-date to stay safe from known vulnerabilities. Don't only look at the operating systems (of your phone and computer) but also the applications and software in those devices.

- **Guard your devices with Antivirus:** Just like how you have a security system at home, put a good antivirus and anti-malware program on your computer to catch and kick out any sneaky viruses. Most Windows PCs come with Defender; make sure it's enabled.

- **Email Smartly:** Be careful when opening emails from strangers. DO NOT click on weird links or download attachments. If someone's asking for your personal or financial info, it's usually a scam; double-check it's legitimate. Don't fall for the urgency, i.e., "act now."

- **Lock Down Your Wi-Fi:** Protect your Wi-Fi network with a strong password. Also, don't use public Wi-Fi for the important stuff; if you have to use public Wi-Fi, **consider using a VPN** for extra security. You know, that thing you have seen in every YouTube video. :)

- **Backup Your Stuff:** It's like having a spare key to your house. Regularly backup your important files and data. That way, you will keep your stuff if something happens.

- **Smart Surfing:** Use secure websites starting with "https://." If a website looks sketchy, do not download anything from it. There are browser extensions that can warn you about unsafe sites.

- **Be Mindful Online:** Think twice before sharing too much on social media. Cyber bad guys can use that info against you. Keep it personal and secure. Those questionnaires on Facebook are the worst for collecting your data.

- **Stay In the Know:** It's like watching the nightly news but for security. Be aware of common online threats and how to protect yourself.

- **Download Carefully:** Get software and apps from trusted sources like official app stores or websites. Avoid those sketchy downloads from unknown companies and sites.

- **Watch your Money:** Regularly check your bank and credit card statements for unfamiliar or unauthorized charges. Report them right away if you spot anything weird.

- **Phone Protection:** Remember your smartphones and tablets. Use screen locks or biometric (fingerprint or face) security, make sure your apps and system are up-to-date, and always back up your data.

- **Turn on that Firewall:** The Online Bouncer: It's like having a bouncer at the door of your online space. Turn on your computer's firewall to block bad stuff from getting in. Also, most Home wifi routers have a simple firewall that you should enable.

- **Protect Your Secrets:** Imagine your data as a treasure chest. Use encryption to keep it safe from prying eyes, whether on your device or being sent online.

- **Clean Out the Junk:** Like decluttering your home, regularly check your computer and phone for unwanted programs or files. Delete what you don't need.

- **Privacy Check:** Take a moment to review your privacy settings on social media. You can control who sees your stuff, so make sure it's only the people you trust.

By taking these proactive steps and maintaining a vigilant mindset, you can create a secure digital environment that protects your personal information and ensures the safety of your online activities. Remember, just as you safeguard your physical home, you can protect your digital life by implementing good cybersecurity practices.

CHAPTER 2

Getting Started in Cybersecurity

Are you ready to get started?

Now that you know what cybersecurity is, about cyber threats and cyber criminals, and some simple strategies to stay safe online, let's talk about how to start learning so you can be part of the next generation of cyber defenders!

If you're new to technology, start by learning the basics of computers and networks, including understanding the different parts of a computer system, like the hardware, software, and operating system. and understanding how networks work, like the different types of networks and the protocols used to communicate over them.

Learning about this will help you both personally and in your cybersecurity journey. Learning about how technology works is integral to learning how to protect it.

Here are some helpful things you can do to learn the basics of computers and networks:

- Take an online course or watch tutorials on YouTube. (There is a wealth of knowledge online that you can take advantage of for free; DON'T BE ASHAMED/ USE IT!)

- Read books and articles on the topic. (Google is your friend!)

- Talk to people who work in IT or cybersecurity. (Join a Study Group/ Non-Profit Support Group)

- Enroll in free webinars provided by various Non-profits on the web.

Once you have a basic understanding of computers and networks, you can start learning more about cybersecurity. As I said, many resources are available online and in libraries to help you get started. **You can do it!**

Now that you are ready and have your primary education completed let's make our plan to set yourself up for success in this exciting field. We will discuss these steps in more detail in the following sections.

- **Start by learning about the basics of cybersecurity**. Including topics such as confidentiality, integrity, and availability, the building blocks of cybersecurity. Network security, information security, and risk management are also great topics to learn about. Free and paid resources are available online and in libraries to help you learn about cybersecurity.

- **Focus on a specific area of cybersecurity.** There are many different areas of cybersecurity, such as network security, application security, and incident response. Choose a focus area of cybersecurity that interests you and focus on developing your skills in that area. (we will be talking about this in the following topic)

- **Start Building a portfolio of cybersecurity projects.** Include personal projects, such as setting up a home network or creating a security blog, or volunteer projects, such as helping a local nonprofit organization with cybersecurity. *All* *of this counts as experience* and **one of the most commonly overlooked items** for new people entering the field.

- **Stay up-to-date on the latest cyber threats and trends.** As you keep up with the news and world events, the cybersecurity world is constantly changing, so staying informed about the latest threats and trends is essential. You can do this by reading cybersecurity blogs and articles and following cybersecurity experts on social media.

What are the different career paths in cybersecurity?

There are many trades in cybersecurity, but the exact number is hard to say because every organization titles its jobs differently, and new technologies always emerge. But some estimates say there are between 50 and 75 different cybersecurity specializations!

In addition to these general trades, there are many more specialized cybersecurity jobs. For example, some people specialize in cloud security, mobile security, or Internet of Things (IoT) security.

What kind of cybersecurity job is right for you? It depends on your interests, skills, and experience. If you need help figuring out where to start, consider talking to a cybersecurity professional or taking a cybersecurity assessment to help you identify your strengths and weaknesses.

In the following sections, we will discuss the different types of specializations and briefly describe what they do.

Defensive Operations

"The Blue Team" is the term for the cybersecurity professionals **defending** organizations from cyber attacks. They do this by monitoring networks and systems for suspicious activity, deploying security controls, educating employees about cybersecurity best practices, and responding to and recovering from cyber incidents.

Here are some examples of what Blue Team members do:

- Monitoring networks and systems for suspicious activity
- Deploying security controls, such as firewalls and intrusion detection systems
- Educating employees about cybersecurity best practices
- Responding to and recovering from cyber incidents

Defensive cybersecurity operations are **critical for protecting organizations** from cyber-attacks. By implementing and maintaining a robust defensive cybersecurity posture, organizations can reduce their risk of becoming victims of cyber attacks.

Here are some **examples** of the jobs in this cybersecurity branch and what they do (**NOTE:** this is not a complete list of all the jobs in this area)

- **Security Operations Analysts:** monitor and protect computer networks from cyberattacks.
- **Network security:** design, implement, and maintain security measures to protect computer networks from cyberattacks.
- **Endpoint security:** protects devices like laptops and smartphones from malware and other threats.
- **Application security:** analyze, inspect, and protect software applications from security vulnerabilities.
- **Data security:** protect the confidentiality, integrity, and availability of data.

- **Identity and access management:** manage user accounts and permissions to ensure only authorized users can access systems and data.

- **Security awareness and training:** educate employees about cybersecurity best practices and how to identify and report suspicious activity.

Blue Team is a great option if you're interested in a cybersecurity career. It's not only a challenging and rewarding field, but it is the **BEST** place for entry-level people, and there's a **VERY high demand for qualified professionals**.

Offensive Operations

"The Red Team" is the term for the cybersecurity professionals responsible for testing the strength of the organization's systems and networks by ethically attacking them. They do this in a controlled environment to help organizations find and fix security vulnerabilities before real-world attackers exploit them.

Red Team members are like the digital equivalent of the bad guys in a movie. They use the same tools and techniques as real-world attackers to gain unauthorized access to systems and networks, steal data, or disrupt operations.

Red Team operations aim **to help** organizations **improve their security posture**. By identifying security vulnerabilities before real-world attackers can exploit them, organizations can reduce their risk of becoming victims of cyber attacks.

These operations test the effectiveness of an organization's security controls and incident response procedures and can help organizations identify and address any weaknesses in their security posture.

Here are some **examples** of jobs in this groups and what they do (**NOTE:** this is not a complete list of all the jobs in this area)

- **Penetration testing:** This involves simulating real-world attacks to identify vulnerabilities in systems and networks.

- **Vulnerability assessment:** This involves identifying and assessing vulnerabilities in systems and networks.

- **Security Red Teaming:** This involves conducting simulated/real-world attacks against an organization's systems and networks to test the effectiveness of its security controls and incident response procedures.

Offensive cybersecurity operations are an essential part of a comprehensive cybersecurity program. By identifying and fixing security vulnerabilities before real-world attackers can exploit them, organizations can reduce their risk of becoming victims of cyber attacks.

IMPORTANT NOTE: offensive cybersecurity operations should only be carried out by **authorized personnel** in a controlled environment. **Unauthorized offensive cybersecurity operations may be illegal and could have serious legal consequences.** That is why when learning, there are training systems called **"ranges"** that you can use to practice these skills safely.

Governance and Risk Management (GRC)

GRC stands for Governance, Risk management, and Compliance. This branch ensures that an organization's cybersecurity activities align with its overall business goals and objectives and comply with relevant laws and regulations.

GRC operations in cybersecurity typically involve the following goals:

- **Identifying and assessing cybersecurity risks** means identifying all the potential threats and vulnerabilities that could affect the organization's cybersecurity. Once the risks have been identified, they are evaluated to determine how likely they are to happen and how much damage they could cause.

- **Developing and implementing cybersecurity policies and procedures** means creating and putting in place rules and processes to help mitigate the identified cybersecurity risks. These policies and procedures should align with the organization's business goals and objectives.

- **Monitoring and reporting on cybersecurity performance** is keeping an eye on the organization's cybersecurity posture and reporting on how it's doing to senior management. This monitoring helps ensure that the organization's cybersecurity program is effective and that any identified risks continue to be managed effectively.

- **Auditing and testing cybersecurity controls** means conducting regular checks of the organization's cybersecurity controls, such as firewalls and intrusion detection systems, to ensure they work as intended.

- **Analyzing cybersecurity incidents** means having plans and procedures for responding to and recovering from cybersecurity attacks. The goal is to minimize the attack's impact and get the organization's systems and data back up and running as quickly as possible.

GRC operations in cybersecurity are a vital part of any comprehensive cybersecurity program. By integrating GRC principles and practices into cybersecurity operations, organizations can improve their security posture, manage risks effectively, and comply with relevant laws and regulations.

With all of these choices, How do I choose my path in Cybersecurity?

Choosing **YOUR** cybersecurity career path can be challenging. There are so many different specializations to choose from! But don't worry, I'm here to help.

When choosing a cybersecurity career path, here are a few things to ask yourself:

- What are you good at? What do you enjoy doing? Consider your strengths and weaknesses. Take inventory of the areas that you are interested in.

- What do you want to achieve in your career? Do you want to be a technical expert, or do you want to be in a management or business role?

- Do you want to work in a specific industry, such as healthcare, infrastructure, or finance?

- What are the job prospects for different cybersecurity roles? Are there jobs in the industry for that specific area?

The **last bullet is critical** when choosing a cybersecurity career path. You want to ensure plenty of jobs are available in your chosen field, and the salaries are competitive.

An excellent resource for this information is the CyberSeek.org Heatmap: https://www.cyberseek.org/heatmap.html. This heatmap shows the demand for different cybersecurity roles in the U.S. It also shows the average salaries for these roles.

It's important to note that job prospects can vary depending on your location and experience level. For example, major metropolitan areas may have more job opportunities than rural ones. And, if you have experience in a specific cybersecurity field, you may have better job prospects than someone just starting their career.

While a job path might sound exciting, there might be few employment opportunities, and you will get discouraged when it's hard to find a job.

When choosing a cybersecurity career path, it's essential to **be realistic** about your job prospects. If you need help deciding which field to choose, talk to experienced cybersecurity professionals. They can give you insights into the job market and help you make an informed decision about your career path.

Once you've thought about these things, you can start researching specific cybersecurity career paths. Many resources are available online and in libraries to help you learn about different cybersecurity roles. You can also talk to cybersecurity professionals who work in the areas that you're interested in.

Here are some things I want you to remember for choosing a cybersecurity career path:

- **Don't be afraid to start small.** You do not need to be an all-around cybersecurity expert to get started in the field. Many entry-level cybersecurity jobs can help you gain experience and develop the skills you need to advance your career, especially in the Blue Team.

- **Your INITIAL CAREER PATH is NOT your entire path!** In my 30+ year career, I have worked in many paths/trades mentioned in the prior sections. **Just because you start on one path doesn't mean you will do it for your entire career.** Remember, you will find your passion when you keep learning, and that passion will translate to a great job.

- **Be willing to learn new things.** The cybersecurity landscape is constantly changing, so it is essential to be ready to learn new things and adapt to new technologies.

- **Get involved in the cybersecurity community.** There are many online and offline cybersecurity communities where you can connect with other professionals, learn about the latest trends and developments in the field, and continue your education.

Choosing your cybersecurity path can be a big decision, but it is crucial. By taking the time to consider your skills, interests, goals, and the job market, you can find the right path for you.

What skills and education do you need to get started in cybersecurity?

Soft Skills/ Power Skills

Let's start with some skills that learners and veterans need to practice and grow constantly. Soft skills, which I call our **"Power Skills."** Power Skills are career-propelling rocket fuel for success in any career, but they are significant in cybersecurity. Cybersecurity professionals must communicate effectively, work in teams, and solve problems creatively. They also need to be able to think critically and make sound decisions under pressure.

Here are some of the essential power skills that supercharge you for success in cybersecurity:

- **Communication:** Cybersecurity professionals must communicate effectively with technical and non-technical audiences. They need to be able to explain complex technical concepts clearly and concisely. They also need to be able to listen to and understand the needs of their team members and stakeholders outside the technology teams.

- **NEVER FORGET that Cybersecurity is a team sport**. Cybersecurity professionals must be able to work effectively with others to identify, assess, and mitigate security risks. They also need to be able to collaborate to develop and implement complex security solutions where only some members have the same knowledge or function.

- **Problem-solving:** Cybersecurity professionals need to be able to think critically and solve problems creatively. They need to be able to analyze complex security problems and develop practical solutions.

- **Critical thinking:** Cybersecurity professionals need to be able to think critically about security risks and threats. They need to be able to evaluate different security solutions and choose the best one for the situation.

- **Decision-making:** Cybersecurity professionals need to be able to make sound decisions under pressure. They often need to make decisions quickly and without the necessary information.

In addition to these Power skills, cybersecurity professionals must have strong technical skills in their chosen path/ trade. However, these POWER skills are just as essential, **if not more so**. Cybersecurity professionals with solid soft skills are **more likely** to succeed.

Don't be discouraged if you still need to develop strong soft skills.

Just like any muscle, these power skills can be exercised and grown.

Here are some of my favorite tips for developing your soft/power skills for a very successful cybersecurity career:

- **Join a Community of interest like Raices Cyber Org.** (https://raicescyber.org | https://www.linkedin.com/company/raicescyberorg) and seek help practicing these and speaking to others about developing yourself.

- **Communication:** Take communication classes or workshops—practice communicating complex technical concepts to non-technical audiences. Prepare small presentations and deliver them in front of others; there is nothing like practicing to improve yourself.

- **Teamwork:** Get involved in extracurricular activities or volunteer work that requires collaboration. Join Capture the Flag (CTF) teams to practice more cyber skills and teamwork concepts. Practice working with others to achieve a common goal.

- **Problem-solving:** Take problem-solving classes or workshops—practice solving problems creatively and developing practical solutions. Getting involved with developing projects will help you work on your portfolio and learn and exercise your problem-solving muscles.

- **Critical thinking:** Take critical thinking classes or workshops. Read Books on the topic and practice evaluating different arguments and choosing the best one.

- **Decision-making:** Take decision-making classes or workshops—practice making decisions under pressure with limited information.

Developing your **POWER** skills can increase your chances of success in this fantastic field. Here are some of my favorite tips for growing your soft skills:

- **Find a mentor.** A mentor can be an invaluable resource for helping you identify where you are weak and to help you develop those soft skills. They can provide guidance and support and help you identify areas you need to improve.

- **Read books and articles about soft skills.** Many resources are available to help you learn about soft skills and how to develop them.

- **Take online courses or workshops.** There are many online courses and workshops available that can teach you about soft skills.

- **Practice, practice, practice!** The best way to develop soft skills is to practice them. Look for opportunities to use your soft skills in work, school, and personal life.

Developing your soft skills takes time and effort, and just so you know, I'm still working on them after three decades, but it is worth it. Cybersecurity professionals with strong soft skills are 125% more likely to be successful in their careers. (I made up that statistic 😃 But you get the picture)

Education

There is **no one right way** to get into cybersecurity. I've been in the field for over 30 years, and I've seen people come in from all different backgrounds. Here are the three most common entry points:

- **Traditional schooling and degrees.** Many people take the traditional route and go to college or university to get a degree in cybersecurity. This can be a good option if you want to learn the fundamentals of cybersecurity and get a well-rounded education.

- **Certifications and training.** Another option is to focus on getting certifications and technical training. This can be a good option if you want to learn specific skills and get into the workforce quickly.

- **Career changers.** Many people already working in IT, such as system administrators, help desk technicians, and hardware support technicians, transition into cybersecurity. This can be a good option if you have relevant skills and experience to apply to cybersecurity.

Whatever your path, the most important thing is to **be passionate** about cybersecurity and **willing to learn**. The field constantly changes, so staying current on the latest trends and technologies is essential.

With the growing demand for cybersecurity professionals, many opportunities are available for people with all experience levels. You can launch a rewarding and in-demand career by developing the skills and knowledge necessary to succeed in cybersecurity.

How do I start learning my chosen path in the field? Resources to Learn

Allow me to begin with this warning!

Be aware of courses that promise to teach you everything you need to know in 90 days. These courses are often scams and very self-promoting; they **will not** give you the skills and knowledge you need to get a job in cybersecurity.

Cybersecurity is a complex and challenging field; regardless of what path you decide to take, it takes **time and effort** to learn the skills you need to be successful. There is **no quick fix**. If you are serious about a career in cybersecurity, be prepared to invest time and effort into your education, knowledge-building, and training.

Many reputable universities and colleges offer cybersecurity degrees and programs. We will be discussing this in the next section. You can also find many online courses and tutorials that can teach you specific skills.

Bootcamps are intensive programs that teach you specific skills or provide reviews quickly. They can be an excellent way to prepare for a certification exam, but you need a deeper understanding of all the cybersecurity concepts you need to succeed in the field. Don't expect a boot camp to teach you everything you need to know about cybersecurity. Use boot camps as a supplement to your knowledge-building and education, not a replacement for it.

Fantastic Training and Certification programs also help you start and focus on your chosen trade path. I will be discussing some of them in the next section.

Now, Let's delve into these details.

Traditional schooling and degrees

Cybersecurity degrees are becoming more commonplace in most 4-year and 2-year academic institutions. This is a very positive development, as it allows students like you to gain a general and comprehensive education in cybersecurity and develop the knowledge to succeed.

One of the biggest challenges for our high school students is that their career counselors and teachers need to learn more about cybersecurity. If they still need to know about the field, how can they tell students it's an option?

When their career counselors need to learn about cybersecurity, Hispanic/Latino students may miss out on learning about this viable career path. Career counselors and educators should learn about cybersecurity, the different career paths and trades, and the many opportunities it offers. This will help them guide all students, especially Hispanic/Latino students, toward a career in cybersecurity if they are interested in the field.

In a 2023 survey of over 300 students enrolled in the Raices Cyber Academy, we found that 86% of students were between the ages of 22 and 41, with over half of them over the age of 31. And more than **76% of all these students were still trying to enter the cybersecurity field**. This indicates that many people are learning about the opportunities in cyber **later in life** because they were unaware that these opportunities existed for them.

These results were a significant shock and surprise to us, and they validated the mission and the issues we're trying to address at Raices Cyber. We're committed to making cybersecurity accessible to everyone, regardless of age, background, or experience.

Another challenge facing Hispanic/Latino students is the **COST** of 4-year degrees. Hispanic/Latino students are more likely to come from low-income families than other racial and ethnic groups in the United States. This can make it difficult for them to afford the high cost of college.

Unfortunately, there is not a lot of financial assistance available specifically for Hispanic/Latino students who want to study cybersecurity post-high school/ secondary school. This can make it hard for Hispanic/Latino students to get the education they need to succeed in this rapidly growing field.

There are a few things that we should be doing to help Hispanic/Latino students overcome all these burdens and challenges of pursuing a degree in cybersecurity:

- First, Creating more scholarships and grants specifically for Hispanic/Latino students in cybersecurity would help level the playing field for this underrepresented group. This would allow more Hispanic/Latino students to pursue a career in cybersecurity, regardless of their financial background. Government agencies, corporations, and philanthropic and nonprofit organizations can all play a role in making cybersecurity more accessible and inclusive by creating more scholarships and grants for Hispanic/Latino students. We can make this field a reality for more students by working together.

- Second, Colleges and universities can create dedicated minority/diversity programs in cybersecurity to provide additional support and resources to Hispanic/Latino students. This could include mentorship programs, tutoring, and career counseling. Colleges and universities can partner with minority-serving institutions (MSIs) and Hispanic-serving institutions (HSIs) to offer joint cybersecurity programs. This would allow Hispanic/Latino students to access high-quality cybersecurity education at their local MSI or HSI. Finally, colleges and universities can work to create a more inclusive and welcoming environment for Hispanic/Latino students in their cybersecurity programs. This could involve culturally responsive teaching practices and creating student organizations and clubs for Hispanic/Latino students in cybersecurity.

- Third, tuition reimbursement programs at companies and businesses can help Hispanic/Latino employees afford a cybersecurity degree, even from low-income families. This can increase the cybersecurity workforce's diversity and make it more representative of the population. Tuition reimbursement programs can also **attract and retain top**

talent. In a competitive job market, offering tuition reimbursement programs can be a way for employers to stand out from the competition and attract the best employees. But we still hear from employers the following; "What if we invest in training our employees, and they leave? Well, I always tell them; what if you don't, and they stay?"

This last point highlights the dilemma many organizations face when deciding whether to invest in the training and development of their employees. However, studies have proven that tuition reimbursement programs can also help improve employee morale and productivity. Employees who feel their employer invests in their education and career development are more likely to be motivated and engaged in their work. Employers can partner with local colleges and universities to offer tuition reimbursement programs to their employees. This can ensure that employees can access high-quality cybersecurity education and complete their degrees while working full-time.

Now that you know some of the challenges and potential solutions that Hispanics/Latinos face while trying to enter the field, let me provide you with some of my favorite strategies and questions you should ask to help you choose a Higher institution for your Degree in Cybersecurity.

Location

- Consider the college's location and whether it is convenient for you to attend. If you plan to work while attending school, choose a college near your job or home. Reduce the friction!

- Don't forget that most colleges also have distance or remote learning options that could be better for your particular lifestyle and work environment.

Curriculum

- Not all University programs are the same. Look for a cybersecurity program that covers a wide range of topics, depending on your professional goals and interests, including the basics of cybersecurity and the electives or specialization you desire. The program should also include hands-on experience, such as labs and internships.

- Choose a curriculum with the areas of specialization you are more drawn to, but be bold and experiment with others; sometimes, we find our passion by doing. Discover your passion by trying new areas out.

Faculty

- Make sure the faculty of the cybersecurity program are experts in the field and have experience in the industry. This will ensure you learn from the best, get the most up-to-date information, and benefit from their expertise.

- Research other activities in the program to see if the university or program hosts guest speakers, career fairs, and conferences.

- Research if the program has clubs and alliances with Non-Profits like Raices Cyber Org. If they do not have these, ask them if they would be open to having a student chapter in their program. This question will be very telling about the programs' flexibility and modernization.

Cost

- Cybersecurity programs can be expensive, so it is essential to factor in the cost of tuition, fees, and living expenses when deciding. Apply for any scholarship programs you can find.

Starting at a Community College

Starting your career in cybersecurity at a local community college is a great way to get started. Community colleges offer affordable, accessible, and flexible cybersecurity programs that can prepare you for success in the field. Below are some of the benefits of doing so:

- Most community colleges now have cybersecurity options for associate degrees (2 years). The benefits of starting in a community college include:

  - Many community colleges offer affordable and high-quality cybersecurity programs. These programs can provide students with the skills and knowledge they need to start a career in cybersecurity without having to take on a lot of student loan debt.

  - Community colleges often have partnerships with local businesses and industries. This can give students opportunities for internships and job shadowing, which can help them gain valuable experience and make connections in the cybersecurity field.

  - Community colleges offer various student support services, such as tutoring, counseling, and career advising. This can be especially helpful for students who are returning to the educational world and are new to cybersecurity or coming from a disadvantaged background.

  - Students can later transfer credits from community colleges to associated four-year colleges and universities, making it easy to continue their education. Many of these colleges partner with other state universities.

A great resource for researching traditional academic organizations is the College Navigator; this website is provided by the National Center for Education Statistics (NCES). It allows you to search for schools by location, degree level, and other criteria. You can also use College Navigator to compare schools and see their graduation rates, job placement rates, and other statistics. https://nces.ed.gov/collegenavigator/

Certifications and Training

Because of the lack of qualified individuals in the cyber world, a brand new focus on non-degree candidate and worker programs is also being seen in the industry as a viable way to bring more people into the field and combat the employment gaps. This is due to the high demand for cybersecurity professionals and the fact that many traditional schooling programs must catch up with the rapidly changing field. Modifying these curricula can be a daunting task for these conventional institutions. Changes and additions of classes can sometimes take over 18 months. That's where Certifications and Specialized training come in.

Non-degree programs can provide students with the skills and knowledge they need to start a career in cybersecurity more quickly and affordably than traditional schooling programs. However, it is essential to note that non-degree programs may be less comprehensive than conventional schooling programs and may lead to different job opportunities.

Free Resources ("cause we love free")

There are many free resources to help you on your journey. YouTube is a goldmine for learning from the pros in the industry, but here's a friendly heads-up: not all advice is created equal. Stick to the "big guns, " those who've earned their stripes. While many

YouTubers are dropping knowledge, some might give outdated or *lousy advice*.

So, when diving into cybersecurity tutorials, keep your radar on thinking critically! Look for the familiar faces, the ones with the certs and the battle scars. You want the real deal: people who've been in the trenches and know their stuff. If you don't know who is in this category, ask! Dive into communities of support and talk to others and those they follow.

Here's the scoop: be very cautious of the so-called *"experts"* who swear you must check off a list of skills before setting foot in the industry. **Cybersecurity isn't a one-size-fits-all kind of gig**. Legit pros get that *everyone's journey is different*.

Instead of stressing over a checklist, focus on building a solid foundation. Get the basics, stay curious, and adapt to the ever-changing scene. And hey, don't be shy – connect with the community, hit up our discord community, and find yourself a mentor who can give you the lowdown tailored to your goals.

Long story short, YouTube's a treasure trove, but your success in cybersecurity hinges on sifting through the noise, tuning into the right voices, and crafting your unique path. Happy learning online!

Many other providers also create excellent content for learning and practicing cybersecurity.

PAID CERTIFICATION PROGRAMS

Over the past three decades, numerous exceptional organizations and companies have played a pivotal role in shaping the educational landscape for professionals in our field. Their commitment to excellence in designing and creating remarkable educational content and programs designed to teach and certify individuals in cybersecurity is evident.

These initiatives have significantly contributed to cultivating a skilled and knowledgeable workforce. The wealth of educational resources, ranging from comprehensive courses to specialized certifications, has empowered individuals to enhance their skill sets and set a standard for excellence in the industry.

Companies such as SANS, CompTIA, EC-Council, TCM-Security, and ISC2, to name a few, have been instrumental in revolutionizing the educational landscape, mainly through their outstanding paid content. These organizations have recognized the critical importance of providing high-quality, specialized materials to professionals seeking to elevate their skills and knowledge in the ever-evolving field of cybersecurity.

SANS, for instance, is renowned for its in-depth and hands-on training programs. Their paid content encompasses courses meticulously designed to address cybersecurity challenges and technologies. The practical focus of SANS training ensures that professionals not only grasp theoretical concepts but also gain valuable real-world experience.

CompTIA has consistently been a trailblazer in IT certifications, offering a comprehensive suite of paid content covering various domains, including cybersecurity. Their certifications, such as Security+ and CySA+, are widely recognized in the industry, providing individuals with a robust foundation and validating their knowledge.

EC-Council is synonymous with ethical hacking and penetration testing certifications. Through their paid content, professionals can delve into the intricacies of offensive security, learning the skills needed to identify and address system vulnerabilities. EC-Council's emphasis on practical, hands-on learning is invaluable in preparing individuals for real-world cybersecurity challenges.

TCM-Security is making waves in the industry by offering practical, scenario-based training through paid content. Their approach focuses on creating an immersive learning experience, allowing professionals to apply their skills in simulated environments. This hands-on methodology enhances comprehension and prepares individuals for the complexities of cybersecurity roles.

ISC2, with its CC, CISSP and other certifications, is a cornerstone in cyber and information security. The paid content offered by ISC2 is renowned for its depth and breadth, covering critical areas such as security architecture and engineering. Professionals engaging with ISC2's content understand cybersecurity principles and practices holistically.

These companies have demonstrated a commitment to excellence in cybersecurity education by investing in premium, paid content. The value lies in the breadth of topics covered and the practical applicability of the knowledge gained. As the cybersecurity landscape continues to evolve, the contributions of organizations like SANS, CompTIA, EC-Council, TCM-Security, and ISC2 remain pivotal in equipping professionals with the skills needed to navigate and excel in this dynamic field.

This is a partial list of all the paid programming available in the educational marketplace. Still, it is a start for people wanting to learn from reputable companies and start their careers.

Put your knowledge to the test and start adding experience to your CV/ Resume.

Experiential training platforms play a crucial role in cybersecurity education by providing hands-on, practical experiences for learners. Below are some of the resources and platforms that you can try out to start your learning; while some focus on Offensive operations

(Pen testing/ red teaming), there are some great resources for other areas:

Hack The Box (HTB): HTB offers a variety of virtual labs and challenges that simulate real-world cybersecurity scenarios. Users can practice penetration testing, ethical hacking, and other cybersecurity skills in a controlled environment.

TryHackMe: TryHackMe is an online platform that provides hands-on labs and exercises for cybersecurity enthusiasts. It covers many topics, including penetration testing, web exploitation, and networking.

OverTheWire: OverTheWire offers online war games designed to teach and practice security concepts. Each game focuses on a specific area, such as cryptography, web security, or system exploitation.

PentesterLab: PentesterLab provides web application security training through practical exercises. Users can learn and practice techniques like SQL injection, cross-site scripting (XSS), and more.

Hacker101: Hacker101 is an educational platform created by HackerOne. It provides free, hands-on training for beginners and experienced individuals, covering web application security and bug bounty hunting topics.

Cybrary Labs: Cybrary offers hands-on labs that cover a range of cybersecurity topics, including penetration testing, incident response, and ethical hacking. These labs provide practical skills and reinforce theoretical knowledge.

Capture the Flag and Other Events

Capture The Flag (CTF) is a cybersecurity competition that challenges participants to solve many security-related tasks and puzzles and challenges them to find "flags" hidden within a system.

These flags may be information, strings, or files that participants need to discover or extract by exploiting vulnerabilities, solving problems, or completing tasks. CTFs simulate real-world cybersecurity scenarios and cover many topics, including cryptography, web security, reverse engineering, forensics, and more.

In a typical CTF, participants, often organized in teams, compete against each other to complete challenges and accumulate points. The challenges are designed to test various skills relevant to cybersecurity, encouraging participants to think critically, analyze complex problems, and exploit vulnerabilities in a controlled environment.

CTFs can occur in various formats, including online platforms where participants connect remotely to servers hosting the challenges or physical events at conferences and cybersecurity competitions. Some CTFs are beginner-friendly, while others are more advanced, catering to participants with varying levels of expertise.

Participating in CTFs is a popular and effective way for individuals to gain hands-on experience, enhance their cybersecurity skills, and stay informed about the latest trends in the field. It also fosters community, as participants often collaborate and share knowledge during and after the competition.

In addition to the Typical CTF, there are other types of competitions that you can participate in.

Social Engineering Competitions

In a social engineering competition, participants undertake simulated scenarios to test and improve their skills in manipulating **human behavior** to gain unauthorized access to information systems or sensitive data. Unlike technical aspects of cybersecurity that focus on exploiting vulnerabilities in technology, **social engineering targets human psychology to exploit trust, authority, or ignorance**.

In a social engineering competition, participants may undertake various challenges such as phishing attacks, impersonation exercises, or scenarios where they attempt to elicit sensitive information through phone calls or in-person interactions. The goal is to assess an individual's ability to manipulate people and extract information without relying on traditional technical exploits.

These competitions serve multiple purposes. They help organizations identify and address weaknesses in their human-centric security measures, such as employee awareness and training programs. For participants, social engineering competitions allow them to refine their social engineering techniques, understand the importance of security awareness, and contribute to the broader field of cybersecurity by promoting better practices to prevent social engineering attacks.

Why should you do this?

Engaging in these activities enriches your skill set and is a valuable addition to bolster your resume/CV, enhancing your appeal to potential employers. Beyond merely showcasing your expertise, these endeavors demonstrate your unwavering spirit and dedication to the field. Employers seek candidates with the right technical know-how and *individuals who exhibit passion and commitment*. Each activity you participate in becomes a testament to your proactive approach, signaling to prospective employers that you go above and beyond in your pursuit of excellence. In a competitive job market, this combination of knowledge, spirit, and dedication becomes a powerful asset, setting you apart as a candidate who understands the field and is genuinely invested in its growth and success.

How do you get the experience that gets you hired?

Getting that first job in cybersecurity can feel like a classic catch-22: you need experience to land a job, but you need a job to gain experience. It's a chicken-and-egg situation. But here's the scoop: *experience is your golden ticket*. Sure, you can hit the books and get all the certifications, and that's fantastic. But when you've rolled up your sleeves and dealt with real-world cybersecurity stuff, it's a game-changer.

Employers want to see that you've been in the trenches, faced challenges, and come out with some battle scars (metaphorical ones, hopefully). It's not just about knowing the theory; it's proving that you can handle the practical, nitty-gritty aspects of the job. So, if you're eyeing that first gig, try to snag internships, **volunteer**, set up your home lab to tinker with things, create, and contribute to public projects. Show them you're not just about the theory; you're ready to bring some hands-on, real-world magic to cybersecurity.

There are many ways I have told my mentees to get experience in cybersecurity before applying for jobs. Here are a few of my favorites:

- **Volunteer for cybersecurity projects.** Many organizations need help with cybersecurity projects. You can volunteer your time to help these organizations with tasks such as conducting security assessments, developing security policies and procedures, or implementing security solutions.

- **Work in an IT support role.** If you can't find a job immediately, try IT support roles. IT support roles can give you valuable experience in troubleshooting computer problems and implementing security solutions. You can also use your IT support role to learn about different types of computer systems and networks.

- **Participate in cybersecurity hackathons.** Cybersecurity hackathons are events where teams of cybersecurity professionals work together to solve cybersecurity challenges. Hackathons are a great way to gain cybersecurity experience and network with other professionals.

- **Contribute to open-source cybersecurity projects.** Many open-source cybersecurity projects need help from volunteers. You can contribute to these projects by writing code, fixing bugs, or testing new features.

- **Take on personal cybersecurity projects.** You can gain experience in cybersecurity by working on personal projects, such as setting up a home network or creating a security blog. You can also use your projects to learn about new cybersecurity tools and technologies.

- **Be willing to learn and experience new things.** The cybersecurity landscape is constantly changing, so it is essential to be ready to learn new things and adapt to new technologies.

- **Get involved in the cybersecurity community.** There are many online and offline cybersecurity communities where you can connect with other professionals and learn about the latest trends and developments in the field.

And there you have it, folks, the lowdown on racking up those first experiences in the cyber universe! Look at it like this: every glitch you troubleshoot, every cyber challenge you tackle—it's like scoring points in your own cybersecurity game. Whether you're rocking in those internships, tinkering in your cyber DIY lab, or jumping into real-world projects, each move is like adding a cool sticker to your cyber skills collection, and you know how much Cyber folks love their stickers. <smiling>

So, pat yourself on the back for those wins, chuckle at the oops moments (trust me, we all have had those oops moments), and gear up for the next level in your cybersecurity journey and make sure you document all of these experiences in your Resume/CV.

Let's hit play on your hands-on, real-world cyber adventure. Get ready because the cyber-rollercoaster is just revving up!

CHAPTER 3

How to find that first job in Cybersecurity

Landing your first gig in cybersecurity WILL feel like navigating a maze, but fear not—it's doable. Like we said before, start by soaking up knowledge like a sponge, understanding the basics, setting up your cyber lab for hands-on experience, and getting certified. Now, get ready to 10x your search by growing your community. **Networking** is your secret weapon; attend meetups, connect with professionals, and don't hesitate to ask for advice. Internships and volunteering are **golden opportunities** to get your foot in the door, so snatch them up. **Tailor your resume** to highlight your cybersecurity skills, even if they come from personal projects. Lastly, showcase your passion, and as I love to say: "Learn in Public," whether it's a blog, a GitHub repository, or presenting in your community or social media.

Employers love candidates with the know-how, passion, and **enthusiasm** to bring to the cyber table. So, gear up, stay persistent, and dive into the cyber job hunt with confidence!

Let's find that first job in Cybersecurity.

Remember that getting that first job will be hard. Be persistent, continue to grow your knowledge, be it your first application or your 100th, stay on course, and don't give up. I promise it will be worth it. While some of these recommendations will start to feel repetitive, see it as a significant highlight of the importance of those recommendations. Now let me give you a few more helpful hints to land that first job:

- **Network with other cybersecurity professionals.** Networking is critical to landing a job in cybersecurity. Attend industry events and conferences, join cybersecurity non-profits, participate in online communities, and actively build your LinkedIn network. In this industry, it's not just about what you know but also about who you know and who knows what you know.

- **Work with a mentor/recruiter.** A mentor is vital when starting your career. A good mentor will help guide you to good recruiters and opportunities that match your personality and goals. Also, partnering with a reputable recruiter can help you identify good cybersecurity jobs that match your skills and experience.

- **Tailor your resume** and cover letter to each job you apply for. Be sure to highlight your relevant skills and experience to the job you are applying for. Tailoring your resume for the position you are applying for is essential as it will help you get through the automated systems and the people evaluating candidates for the positions. Make it clear that you have the skills they are looking for.

- **Prepare for job interviews.** Practice answering common cybersecurity interview questions. You can find many resources online and in books to help you prepare for job interviews. Find that community and set up Mock Interviews. These practice interviews are also invaluable to help you prepare for those challenging experiences.

Job Searching in Cybersecurity for People Already in the Field

Navigating a career change from another IT field to cybersecurity can be a smoother transition than finding that first job, as you bring experience and skills to the table. However, it's crucial to approach your job search with a proactive and strategic mindset. Also, follow the steps outlined in the previous chapter to navigate this transition effectively.

Here are some tips I have used in my career that will help you find that next job as you move into cybersecurity:

- **Update your resume and cover letter.** Be sure to highlight all your brand-new skills, certifications, and experience in cybersecurity. You can also use your resume and cover letter to explain why you are looking for a new job and what you are looking for in your next role.

- **Network with cybersecurity professionals.** Networking is an invaluable tool in the cybersecurity job hunt. While technical expertise is crucial, **the power of personal connections can't be underestimated**. Actively engage in industry events and online forums, and leverage LinkedIn to expand your network. Let your contacts know about your career aspirations and be receptive to potential opportunities that may arise through these connections. Just as you learn in public, make that job search known to the public. You never know who may be looking for someone just like YOU.

- **Seeking guidance from a mentor is a timeless career advancement strategy,** regardless of stage or experience level. A mentor's insights, expertise, and connections can be invaluable assets as you navigate the ever-evolving professional landscape. Whether you're a seasoned professional seeking a new challenge or an aspiring individual just starting, a mentor can provide valuable support and guidance. They can help you identify new opportunities that align with your skills and aspirations, expand your professional network, and navigate career transitions effectively. Mentorship is a two-way street, and both parties can benefit from the relationship. As you gain from your mentor's wisdom and experience, you also have the opportunity to learn and grow alongside them, contributing your unique perspectives and knowledge. Embarking on a mentorship journey is an investment in your professional and personal growth. It's always possible to tap into the power of mentorship and unlock a world of new possibilities.

- **Prepare for job interviews.** Sharpen your interview skills by practicing common cybersecurity interview questions. Leverage the wealth of online resources and books to enhance your preparation. Engaging in **mock interviews** with mentors and friends in the field can also prove invaluable in refining your responses under pressure.

Here are some other valuable tips that I have used in my career:

- **Be specific about what you are looking for.** Are you looking for a job within a particular area of cybersecurity, such as security operations, security engineering, vulnerability analysis, governance, or application security? Are you seeking a job in a specific industry, such as healthcare, finance, or infrastructure protection? Be as straightforward as possible in your job search so that you can find the right job for you. The concept of "Spray and Pray" can be practical sometimes in finding "a job" but may not get you "the job" that YOU are looking for.

- **Be flexible.** Maintaining flexibility is critical to expanding your career prospects. If you live in an area with few jobs, consider relocating or looking in other geographical areas to increase your job opportunities. Additionally, as a newcomer to the field, be open to adjusting your salary expectations. You **will not** get that six-figure salary in your first job. Remember the adage: "it's easier to find a job when you have one." Secure that initial position, hone your skills for a few years, and then pursue your targeted job.

- **Don't give up.** Let me say it **out loud so everyone can hear me:** "you will not get the first job you interview for; you might not get the first 20 jobs you interview for". **Finding a job can be challenging**, but it is essential to stay positive and persistent. Keep networking, applying for jobs, and preparing for interviews. You will find that job, and you will be better for it! **DON'T GIVE UP!**

Launching your cybersecurity career can be a thrilling adventure filled with opportunities for growth and fulfillment. By following the tips we've covered, you'll be well on your way to landing a job that sparks your passion and allows you to continuously expand your skills and expertise, not only for you but for the entire community. Imagine yourself tackling cutting-edge cybersecurity challenges and making a real impact in the world – that's the exciting reality that awaits you!

How to network the right way

Networking with fellow professionals is a 10x strategy for career advancement, knowledge exchange, and collaborative problem-solving. As robust security systems protect against cyber threats, a solid professional network safeguards your career growth and opens new opportunities. By cultivating meaningful connections with peers, mentors, and industry experts, you gain access to invaluable insights, expand your professional horizons, and position yourself as a sought-after cybersecurity professional.

There are many ways to network with other cybersecurity professionals. Here are some of my favorite tips:

- **Join online communities.** There are many online communities for cybersecurity professionals, such as LinkedIn groups, forums, and Discord servers. These communities are a great way to connect with other cybersecurity professionals worldwide and discuss topics of interest. Selfishly, I recommend our Raices Cyber Org Discord server, where you can find people worldwide in all stages of their careers. We have folks just starting as well as seasoned Industry professionals with decades of experience in cybersecurity. (https://discord.gg/raicescyber)

- **Attend industry events.** Many cybersecurity conferences, meetups, and other events are held throughout the year. These events are a great way to meet other cybersecurity professionals and learn about the latest trends and developments in the field. Again, Raices Cyber Org has over 20 City Chapters in the US and 3+ City Chapters outside the US. These chapters hold virtual and In-person monthly educational meetups/networking activities that you can attend free of charge. For more information on these events, follow our LinkedIn. (https://www.linkedin.com/company/raicescyberorg)

- **Reach out to people on LinkedIn.** If you see a cybersecurity professional on LinkedIn that you admire or who you think could be a valuable connection, **follow them**, learn from them, see what events they are going to, comment on their posts, and establish a professional relationship via those posts **before you send them a message**. Once established, send them a personalized message introducing yourself and explaining why you want to connect with them. You will see that most of the good people out there are more than willing to connect and share their stories and support with those who are truly dedicated and professional in their approach.

- **Contribute to open-source projects.** Open-source projects are a great way to collaborate with other cybersecurity professionals and learn from them. You can also use your contributions to open-source projects to demonstrate your skills and expertise to potential employers.

- **Write a blog or create videos about cybersecurity.** Again, **learn in PUBLIC** and share your experiences and your challenges. You never know how your own experience will help others. This is also a great way to demonstrate your expertise in cybersecurity and thought leadership expertise. It can also help you to connect with other cybersecurity professionals interested in the same topics.

Just like we exercise our physical muscles, we also need to develop and regularly use our **"soft skills," which I also call "power skills."** These skills are often even more important than technical skills, and here are some additional tips that I believe in my heart are essential for success:

- **Be genuine and authentic.** People can tell when you are being fake, so be yourself and be sincere in your interactions with other cybersecurity professionals.

- **Be helpful and supportive.** Offer to help other cybersecurity professionals with their problems or questions. The idea of **'each one, teach one'** is like a secret superpower that can change lives, communities, and even the world. It's saying, 'Hey, I know something, and I'm going to share it with you so you can learn and grow, too.' And when we all do that, we create a world where knowledge is like a flowing river accessible to everyone. **Imagine a world where learning isn't just for the lucky few** but for everyone who wants to learn, where knowledge is shared freely and openly, like a gift from one person to another. And where everyone has the chance to reach their full potential. **That's the kind of world I want to create by embracing the 'each one, teach one' principle.**

- **Be respectful of everyone's time.** Don't be afraid to ask for help, but be mindful of other people's time and respect their boundaries.

- **Follow up.** If you meet someone at an event or online, follow up afterward. Send a message thanking the person for their time or connecting with them on LinkedIn.

Networking with other cybersecurity professionals can help you learn new things, find job opportunities, and build a successful career. Following the tips above, you can start networking with other cybersecurity professionals and creating unique and fulfilling relationships that will benefit you throughout your career.

How to stay up-to-date on the hottest cybersecurity trends and threats

The cybersecurity landscape is changing every day, and it's a vast ecosystem. This large environment can be daunting, especially for newcomers. But fear not, fellow cyber enthusiasts! With a sprinkle of curiosity and a dash of determination, you can stay ahead of the curve and keep your cybersecurity knowledge sharp. Here are some great examples of staying on top of this dynamic field's latest trends and threats.

- **Read cybersecurity news, blogs, and articles.** There are many high-quality cybersecurity blogs and articles available online. These resources can help you to learn about the latest trends and threats in cybersecurity.

- **Follow cybersecurity experts on social media.** Many cybersecurity experts are active on social media, such as Twitter ("X"), mastodon, Instagram, threads, and LinkedIn. Following these experts can help you stay up-to-date on cybersecurity's latest developments (*and events*).

- **Attend cybersecurity conferences and events.** Cybersecurity conferences and events are a great way to learn about the latest trends and threats in cybersecurity and network with other cybersecurity professionals. Webinars are also great for learning new techniques, technologies, and topics.

- **Take cybersecurity courses and training.** There are many cybersecurity courses and training programs available online and in person. These courses and training programs can help you develop the skills and knowledge to protect yourself and your organization from cyber threats. **IMPORTANT NOTE:** Not every course you take has to be a "Certificate Generating event"; take courses for the satisfaction of learning, and take classes when interested in a specific topic. This will help make you a more rounded cybersecurity professional, and you may discover your passion for a topic you didn't plan on.

- **Read official cybersecurity reports.** Cybersecurity reports can provide valuable insights into the latest trends and threats in cybersecurity. Some popular cybersecurity reports include the Verizon Data Breach Investigations Report and the IBM X-Force Threat Intelligence Index.

How to continue to develop your cybersecurity skills

I've been practicing in this field for over three decades, and let me tell you, the world of cybersecurity has changed dramatically since I first started. Back then, we were using technology that is currently featured in some museums, which would seem like ancient relics today! But here's the thing to remember: if I hadn't been constantly learning and adapting, I wouldn't have been able to keep up with these changes and stay relevant in this ever-evolving industry. Continuous learning is not just an option in cybersecurity; **it is a must** to remain relevant in this field. **Never Stop Learning!**

Keeping your skills sharp is like maintaining an airplane. It needs regular maintenance to keep flying; your cybersecurity knowledge needs continuous nurturing to stay ahead of evolving technologies, threats, and trends.

There are many ways to develop your cybersecurity skills continuously. Here are a few of the strategies I follow (and yes, I said these before, but they are **THAT** important):

- **Continue to take cybersecurity courses and training.** There are many cybersecurity courses and training programs available online and in person. These courses and training programs can help you develop the skills and knowledge to protect yourself and gain valuable self-improvement knowledge. *Remember, not all education needs to lead to certification; enroll* in non-certification courses, webinars, and presentations to keep your skills sharp.

- **Read new cybersecurity books and articles.** There are many high-quality cybersecurity books and articles available and upcoming. These resources can help you learn about the latest trends and threats in cybersecurity and enhance your knowledge.

- **Follow cybersecurity experts on social media and Online.** Many cybersecurity experts are active on social media, such as Twitter and LinkedIn. Following these experts can help you to stay up-to-date on the latest developments in cybersecurity.

- **Attend cybersecurity conferences and events.** Cybersecurity conferences and events are a great way to learn about cybersecurity trends and threats and network with other cybersecurity professionals.

- **Volunteer with organizations helping others.** There is no better way to learn than to teach and share your knowledge.

Additionally, there are other significant things to keep in mind if you want to grow your career:

- **Set goals for yourself.** What cybersecurity skills do you want to develop? Once you know what you want to learn, you can create a plan to achieve your goals.

- **Find a mentor.** A mentor can provide you with guidance and support as you develop your cybersecurity skills.

- **Be patient and persistent.** Developing cybersecurity skills takes time and effort. Don't get discouraged if you don't master everything right away. Just keep learning and practicing, and you will eventually reach your goals.

Continuing to Develop your cybersecurity skills is a significant **investment in your future**. Following the tips above, you can maintain the skills and knowledge needed to increase your personal and professional value. **Never Stop Learning!**

CHAPTER 4

Passion, Hard Work, and Humility: The Keys to Success in Cybersecurity

As you have heard me say in this book, Cybersecurity is a challenging and rewarding field. In all my years in this line of work, I have observed that those who succeed in it share a few key traits: passion for the work, a strong work ethic, and a humble attitude.

This chapter will explore these traits in more depth and discuss how they can help you achieve your cybersecurity career goals.

Passion: Cybersecurity is a complex and ever-evolving field, so it is essential to be passionate about the work to *stay motivated and engaged*. If you are not passionate about cybersecurity, staying up-to-date on the latest threats and technologies will be difficult, and you will likely burn out quickly.

Hard work: Cybersecurity is also a very demanding field. There is always more to learn, and you must be willing to work hard to stay ahead of the curve. This means being ready to study new technologies, attend conferences, and network with other professionals.

Humility: No matter your experience or knowledge, there is always more to learn in cybersecurity. It is essential to be humble and always be willing to admit when you don't know something. Like my father taught me long ago: "...as for me, all I know is that I know nothing" - Socrates. There is much to learn, and no one knows everything. Keep this phrase in mind, and continue learning and growing professionally.

If you can **cultivate** these three traits, you will be well on your way to success in your cybersecurity career. **To cultivate something is to nurture it and help it grow to its full potential.** It describes both physical and intangible things. Cultivation takes time and effort. It requires regular attention and care. But the rewards of cultivation can be significant. When you cultivate something, you help it to become better and stronger.

I know I did. When I first started in security in the late 80's, I was clueless, along with all my peers. Technology was still in its infancy; the internet as we know it was just dial-up via phone lines to bulletin boards and forums. But I was passionate about learning and eager to make a difference. So, I buckled down and studied everything I could about technology. I learned how it worked, how it could break, and what could happen. I spoke to professors and researchers in the field, read books and articles, and talked to other professionals.

At first, it was tough. There was so much to learn, and I always felt overwhelmed. But I didn't give up. I kept working hard and learning as much as I could. I made it a game; I loved to learn, I loved technology.

Over time, my skills and knowledge grew. I started getting more involved in the security community, experimenting with new technology, and trying things out; that is the original definition of a hacker. Back then, a hacker was a person who enjoyed learning about technology and how to use it in new and distinct ways.

Hackers were often skilled in programming, computer hardware, and learning new technologies. They used their skills to solve problems, build new things, and explore the incredible possibilities of technology. I wanted to do that, and after I did, and because of that, I started to land more challenging and rewarding jobs. At that time, there were no jobs specifically for security; we were all technologists who helped in various ways, and we "created our security jobs."

After 34 years, I'm still cultivating the learning, and **yes,** I still have the passion. But I know I wouldn't be where I am today without that passion for the work, my work ethic, and my humble attitude. This last one took years to perfect and was the hardest to learn.

If you're interested in an enriching career in cybersecurity, **I encourage you never to stop cultivating!**

Be passionate about Cybersecurity.

Passion is a mighty force that can drive you to achieve great things. The fire that burns deep inside you fuels you to keep going. If you are passionate about cybersecurity, you will be more likely to stay motivated and engaged in your career. You will also be more likely to go the extra mile to learn new things and stay ahead of the curve.

Sometimes, we need to learn how to become passionate, and becoming more passionate about your work takes time and effort, but it's worth it. When you're passionate about your work, you're more likely to be successful and happy in your career.

Why should you ignite the passion? Let me tell you about some of the ways that being passionate about cybersecurity can help you succeed in your career:

1. **You will be more motivated to learn and grow.** When you are passionate about something, you are more likely to be

curious and eager to learn new things. This is essential in cybersecurity, where the field constantly evolves; you need to know new things, tactics, techniques, and technology, and new threats always emerge.

2. **You will be more likely to go the extra mile.** When you are passionate about your work, you are more likely to go above and beyond what is expected. This can put you ahead of the competition and make you more attractive to potential employers.

3. **You will be more engaged and productive.** You are more likely to be engaged and effective when you are passionate about your work. This is because you are more likely to find your work meaningful and rewarding.

4. You will be less likely to burn out. When you are passionate about a topic, learning and doing things on that topic are things that you WANT to do versus things that you HAVE to do.

If you are not sure if you already have the cybersecurity fire, ask yourself these questions:

- Do I like figuring out what happened in that last hack I read on the internet or saw on the news? Do I enjoy learning about new technologies and new threats?

- Do I like puzzles? Do I like mysteries, and am I driven to solve them? Am I interested in solving complex problems?

- Am I excited about making a difference in the world by improving safety, eliminating risks, and protecting my family, community, and nation with cybersecurity?

If you answered **yes** to any of these questions, then you are on your way to being passionate about cybersecurity.

Here are some more of my recommendations for growing and cultivating your passion for cybersecurity:

Read and Stay up-to-date on the latest cybersecurity trends and threats. There are many ways to do this, such as reading cybersecurity books, blogs, and articles, watching your favorite cybersecurity YouTube creators, and listening to informative security podcasts.

Get involved in the cybersecurity community. I can't say this enough: joining cybersecurity professional organizations is a significant part of igniting that flame inside. After attending meetups or conferences, I am always "fired up" and want to do more!

Find a mentor or a MasterMind Group. A mentor can help you learn more about cybersecurity and provide guidance and support. Form accountability or MasterMind groups to help you guide and motivate you because we all need that support and push when things get tough.

Get involved in cybersecurity projects. There are many ways to do this, such as volunteering for your local cybersecurity organization or participating in open-source projects.

By following these tips, you can cultivate and grow your passion for your career and life in cybersecurity and set yourself up for success. **Let's ignite that fire within!**

Be willing to work hard.

Let us not sugarcoat it: Cybersecurity **is a HARD and demanding field**, and it is crucial to be willing to work hard to succeed. This means working long hours, learning new things quickly, and adapting to change. Some people say that Cybersecurity is not a career; it's a lifestyle.

There are a few reasons why cybersecurity is such a demanding field. First, the field is constantly changing, evolving as new technology and business methods emerge. New threats are emerging all the time, and cybersecurity professionals need to be able to stay up-to-date on the latest trends and threats. Second, cybersecurity is complex, and professionals must deeply understand various technologies. Third, cybersecurity is a high-stakes field. Mistakes **can have serious consequences**, so cybersecurity professionals need to be able to work under pressure and make sound decisions quickly.

Despite the challenges, **cybersecurity is a highly enriching field**. Cybersecurity professionals like you are critical in protecting our world from cyber threats. They also have the opportunity to work on cutting-edge technologies and solve complex problems.

If you are willing to work hard, **you can succeed in cybersecurity**. So, how do we do this:

- **Be willing to learn new things quickly.** Cybersecurity is a rapidly changing field, so it is essential to *be ready to learn* new things quickly. Many resources are available to help you learn about cybersecurity, such as books, articles, online courses, and conferences.

- **Be proactive.** Cybersecurity professionals need to be proactive in their approach to security. This means identifying and addressing potential threats before they become problems. Sometimes, the alert person reads something on Twitter ("X") that raises the alarm before it's discovered in your environment. Call it Out!

- **Be detail-oriented.** Cybersecurity professionals need to be detail-oriented in their work. Small mistakes can have serious consequences.

- **Be able to work under pressure.** Cybersecurity professionals often need to work under pressure, dealing with high-stakes situations.

- **Be able to think critically. "Question everything".** Cybersecurity professionals need to be able to think critically and solve complex problems. This is because they often need to develop new and innovative solutions to security challenges.

If you are willing to work hard and develop the skills and knowledge necessary to succeed, you can also have a gratifying cybersecurity career.

Be Humble

Humility is an essential quality for success in cybersecurity. As I have said in this book, Cybersecurity is a complex and ever-evolving field, and **no one knows everything**. It is vital to be humble and willing to learn from others. There are **NO EXPERTS IN THE ENTIRE FIELD** of Cybersecurity. We are all learning and practicing our skills as we go.

There are a few essential reasons why humility is so vital in cybersecurity. First, **cybersecurity is a team sport**. Cybersecurity professionals need to be able to collaborate with others and share their knowledge. Humility is essential for effective collaboration.

Second, cybersecurity is a constantly changing field. New threats are emerging all the time, and cybersecurity professionals need to **be willing to admit that they don't know everything**. Humility allows cybersecurity professionals to be open to new ideas and to learn from their mistakes. Remember, "You learn more from failure than you will ever from success."

Third, cybersecurity is a high-stakes field. Mistakes can have serious consequences. Humility helps cybersecurity professionals be mindful of the risks and take the necessary precautions. Ask before you do, and don't be too proud to ask for help.

Here are a few of my tips for being and staying humble in cybersecurity:

- **Be willing to admit when you don't know something**. It's okay not to know everything. The important thing is to be ready to learn new skills.

- **Be open to feedback and give constructive feedback.** Feedback is a gift. It's an opportunity to learn and grow.

- **Be willing to collaborate with others.** Cybersecurity is a *team sport*. Share your knowledge and learn from others.

- **Give credit where credit is due. When** others help, be sure to give them credit.

It is vital to reinforce that humility is a critical skill that will help you succeed in cybersecurity, both in your learning and career. It will make you a better team player, a better learner, and a better decision-maker. Humility is not just for learners and students; teachers, leaders, and veterans must be humble.

In this chapter, we have explored the three keys to success in cybersecurity: passion, hard work, and humility. Passion will drive you to learn and grow, even when things are tough. Hard work will help you develop the skills and knowledge you need to succeed. And humility will keep you grounded and open to learning from others.

If you can cultivate these three traits, you will be well on your way to success in cybersecurity. It is a challenging but rewarding field, and there is always more to learn. But with passion, hard work, and humility, you can achieve your goals and make a difference.

As we look to the future of cybersecurity, it is essential to remember that we know that we are all in this together. We must collaborate to share knowledge, develop new solutions, and protect our world from cyber threats. By embracing the three keys to success in cybersecurity, we can create a safer and more secure future for all.

The future of cybersecurity is bright. The need for cybersecurity professionals will only grow as the world becomes increasingly digitized. If you are passionate about cybersecurity, hard-working, and humble, you will have many opportunities to grow and make a difference.

I encourage you to pursue your dreams in cybersecurity. It is a field that offers the chance to learn, grow, and make a positive impact on the world.

CHAPTER 5

Resources for Latinos in Cybersecurity

As discussed earlier in this book, it is estimated that **only 4%** of the current cybersecurity workforce self-identifies as Hispanic, Latino, Latina, or LatinX. In this section, we will discuss the birth of our organization, why we need to focus on this underrepresented group, and what we can all do to support each other regardless of race, color, creed, etc.

The Birth of RAICES CYBER ORG: *The First Organization for Latinos in Cybersecurity in the USA!*

It was the summer of 2021, and the world was slowly emerging from the grip of the COVID-19 pandemic. Activities, conferences, and events were cautiously reopening their doors, and I was "hunkered down" in my home office outside Philadelphia, PA. One day, I received a message from a group of friends who had just attended a conference. Their words struck a chord: "Eric, we saw only a handful of Hispanics at this conference. We have to do something about this." My initial response was a hesitant, "Yeah, that's par for the course," but that conversation got me thinking.

I looked back at the first 20 years of my career and realized no one else looked like **me.** In all my jobs and the teams I worked in, I seldom encountered another Latino; when you did, you would gravitate to each other somehow. Later, when I grew into leadership positions, I was usually the only Hispanic/ Latino in most leadership meetings. Even nowadays, when you see another Latino in the workplace, your eyes light up, and you smile and nod.

But, like I said, this got my wheels turning. I reached out to a few friends in academia. I asked them to research if there were any existing organizations dedicated to helping our community of Hispanics and Latinos get into the field of cybersecurity. After a few days, their answer came: **NONE**. There were no unique organizations in the USA dedicated to this mission. There were organizations for Latinos In Tech, Latinos in Code, Latinos in Web, Hispanics in Tech, etc., and within each of those there were communities of support for cyber. Still, no dedicated organization existed to support Hispanics, Latinos, Latinas, and LatinX in Cybersecurity.

Their research showed that only 4% of the US cyber workforce self-identified as Hispanic/Latino. **4%**, a number that gnawed at me and became **my war cry**.

The evening after that meeting, I posted a simple message on Twitter: "If I build this organization, would you come?" and went to bed. The following day, hundreds of people had liked, shared, and commented on that post. It was then that I knew what I had to do.

Never in my wildest dreams did I imagine myself as a "social justice warrior." I didn't even have a passing interest in it. In fact, throughout my career, I actively avoided anything that could be perceived as activism towards my heritage. My motto was: 'Just be better than the average person, and you'll succeed. But a fire was lit in my soul!

In the quiet solitude of my home office, a stark "4%" tugged from the depths of my soul, boldly etched onto a plain sheet of paper that

I had taped upon my wall. This haunting number, a stark reminder of the abysmal representation of Hispanics in the cybersecurity realm, was a constant reminder of the mission that I had to do.

For three days, I poured my heart and soul into this endeavor, fueled by an unwavering realization that this was my calling. Raices Cyber, a beacon of hope and opportunity, was born from the ashes of injustice and apathy.

This wasn't merely a side project; it embodied my most profound purpose, a calling that resonated within the core of my being. With each passing moment, my resolve grew more vigorous, ignited by an insatiable hunger to shatter that glass ceiling and uplift my fellow Hispanics and Latinos to their rightful place in the cybersecurity landscape.

Raices Cyber was not born out of a desire for recognition or accolades but from a profound yearning to make a difference, empower others to reach their full potential, shatter stereotypes, and pave the way for a brighter future. It was a testament to the indomitable human spirit of this community, a symbol of hope in a world desperately in need of change.

The "Why?"

With that realization that Hispanics, Latinos, Latinas, and Latinx had such an abysmal representation in this field, my thoughts shifted to the "why." Why is it so hard for our people to achieve in this field? I needed to know if I was to make a difference. As I researched and discussed with others, I saw some troubling patterns emerge.

Lack of direction and understanding in the field: The absence of clear guidance and insufficient knowledge about cybersecurity among Hispanic/Latino students significantly impacts their career paths. Often, these students, educators, and career counselors must be educated about the vast cybersecurity opportunities and rewarding careers available. Educators and Career Counselors must usually be educated to inform the students about the over 50 career paths and trades in the field.

Scarcity of Hispanic/Latino role models in cybersecurity: The underrepresentation of Hispanic/Latino professionals in cybersecurity further perpetuates the need for more awareness among students. Role models serve as **powerful motivators** and provide valuable insights into the field, which are often absent in the lives of Hispanic/Latino students. Students, and all of us, want to see ourselves represented in a field in which we seek to belong.

Cultural and linguistic barriers: Cultural and linguistic barriers can hinder Hispanic/Latino students' access to information and opportunities in cybersecurity. Language disparities in educational materials and a lack of culturally sensitive outreach can discourage students from pursuing careers in cybersecurity.

Limited exposure to cybersecurity education and resources: Hispanic/Latino students often need access to quality cybersecurity education and resources within their communities and educational institutions. This results in a gap in their understanding of the field and its potential career prospects. This is due to several factors, including districts with poor educational resources, poverty, lack of transportation, cultural bias, and, in some cases, discrimination.

Financial barriers: The cost of education and training in cybersecurity is often prohibitive for many Latinos. This especially true for Latinos who come from low-income families.

Stereotypes and misconceptions about cybersecurity: Misconceptions about cybersecurity as a male-dominated or highly technical field can deter Hispanic/Latino students from exploring it as a career option. These stereotypes can create unnecessary self-doubt and hinder students from recognizing their potential in the field. The field of cybersecurity is not only for the "STEM" crowd; this field has something for everyone.

What can we do?

Effectively addressing the underrepresentation of Hispanics/Latinos in cybersecurity requires a comprehensive and multifaceted approach encompassing various educational and professional development aspects. This approach must provide access to quality cybersecurity education and resources, promote Hispanic/Latino representation, address cultural and linguistic barriers, and actively challenge stereotypes and misconceptions about cybersecurity careers.

- **Increasing access to cybersecurity education and resources:** Expanding access to quality cybersecurity education and resources in underserved communities and educational institutions is crucial to raising awareness among Hispanic/Latino students. This includes providing culturally relevant and accessible educational materials, offering hands-on learning opportunities, and establishing mentorship programs.

- **Promoting Hispanic/Latino representation in cybersecurity:** Actively highlighting successful Hispanic/Latino cybersecurity professionals and role models can significantly impact the perception of the field among students and their communities. This can be achieved through media campaigns, including talks in high schools and universities, showcasing the achievements of Hispanic/Latino cybersecurity professionals, and creating a network of mentors and advisors.

- **Addressing cultural and linguistic barriers:** Tailoring cybersecurity education and outreach to the specific cultural and linguistic needs of Hispanic/Latino students is essential to dismantling barriers. This involves translating educational materials into Spanish, providing culturally sensitive guidance, and incorporating culturally relevant examples into teaching strategies.

- **Challenging stereotypes and misconceptions:** Actively dispelling stereotypes and misconceptions about cybersecurity can help create a more inclusive and welcoming environment for Hispanic/Latino students. This involves highlighting the diverse range of career paths within the field, emphasizing the value of cultural perspectives, and providing opportunities for students to interact with cybersecurity professionals from different backgrounds.

By addressing these issues and implementing targeted initiatives, we can effectively guide Hispanic/Latino students toward fulfilling careers in cybersecurity, enabling them to contribute their unique skills and perspectives to this critical field.

Professional organizations and communities for Hispanics/Latinos in cybersecurity

As of the time this book was written, only a few organizations support the community with active programs. Here are some of my favorite organizations and communities for Latinos in cybersecurity that you should investigate:

- **Raíces Cyber Org** is a non-profit organization that aims to empower and support the Hispanic and Latino cyber and technology community. We provide various resources, including education, scholarships, events and activities, mentorships, and networking opportunities.

- **Cyversity** is a non-profit organization dedicated to diversifying the cybersecurity workforce. They provide various resources, including scholarships, mentorships, networking opportunities, and professional development training, to underrepresented minorities, including women and Hispanics/Latinos. Cyversity's mission is to "achieve the consistent representation of women, underrepresented minorities, and all veterans in the cybersecurity industry through programs designed to diversify, educate, and empower."

- **Minorities in Cybersecurity (MiC)**: MiC is a non-profit organization that provides practical knowledge, training, development, and support to minorities interested in cybersecurity careers. They also offer a variety of resources, including webinars, conferences, and a job board.

- **SOMOS.tech** (We are tech): SOMOS.tech is a non-profit organization that promotes the advancement of Latinos/Latinas in technology. They provide various resources, including scholarships, internships, mentorships, and networking opportunities.

- **Techqueria:** Techqueria is a non-profit organization that serves the largest global community of Latinx professionals in tech. They provide various resources, including career guidance, networking opportunities, and events.

- **LatinX DLN, or LatinX Digital Leaders Now**, is dedicated to increasing Latino representation in technology-related careers and ensuring their voices are heard in developing and implementing technology policies. They work to bridge the digital divide by providing access to education, resources, and opportunities for Latinos in the tech industry.

- **WOMCY, also known as Latam Women in Cybersecurity**, is a non-profit organization dedicated to empowering and supporting women in the cybersecurity field in Latin America. WOMCY has a mission to "minimize the knowledge gap and increase the talent pool in cybersecurity in Latin America."

- **Girl Security** is a non-profit organization that promotes the inclusion and advancement of girls, women, and gender minorities (ages 14-26) in the security sector. Through a pathways approach, Girl Security advances historically underrepresented populations across the public and private sectors, leveraging early-stage mentorship, financially supported workforce training, and supportive services.

In addition to these organizations, there are several other online and in-person communities for Latinos in cybersecurity. For example, there are some Spanish-language cybersecurity blogs and websites. There are also some cybersecurity conferences and events that offer Spanish-language sessions.

In addition to the previous Hispanic Serving Organizations, other Diversity partner organizations actively work with Raices Cyber and support this great community:

- **Black Girls Hack** is a non-profit organization dedicated to increasing the representation of Black women in cybersecurity. They provide various resources, including scholarships, internships, mentorships, and networking opportunities, to help Black women succeed in the tech industry.

- **Women in Cybersecurity (WiCyS)**: WiCyS is a global non-profit organization that empowers women to pursue, excel, and advance in cybersecurity careers. They provide various resources, including scholarships, internships, mentorships, and networking opportunities.

- **The Women's Society of Cyberjutsu (WSC)** is a non-profit organization dedicated to empowering women to succeed in the cybersecurity industry. WSC has a mission to "advance women in cybersecurity careers by providing programs and partnerships that promote hands-on training, networking, education, mentoring, resource-sharing, and other professional opportunities."

By getting involved with these professional organizations and communities, Hispanics, Latinos, Latinas, and LatinX in cybersecurity can connect with other professionals, learn new skills, and advance their careers.

Scholarships and financial aid programs for Latinos interested in cybersecurity

Financial aid and access to educational resources are invaluable in the field. Almost every organization from the past chapter offers quality education and resources to its members. In addition to these organizations, here are some additional resources to research:

- UMSA Foundation Scholarship: The UMSA Foundation Scholarship is a $3,000 scholarship awarded to a Latino student pursuing a degree in cybersecurity. The scholarship is renewable for up to four years.

- WSOS Baccalaureate Scholarship: The WSOS Baccalaureate Scholarship is a $22,500 scholarship awarded to a Latino student pursuing a degree in cybersecurity. The scholarship is renewable for up to four years.

- Elms College STEM Scholarships: Elms College offers a variety of STEM scholarships, including the Elms Cyber

Scholarship, which awards $40,000 per year to a Latino student pursuing a degree in cybersecurity.

- CyberCorps® Scholarship for Service (SFS): The CyberCorps® Scholarship for Service (SFS) is a scholarship and service program that awards up to $20,000 per year to students pursuing a degree in cybersecurity. In return for the scholarship, recipients must agree to work for a government agency for at least three years after graduation.

- National Science Foundation (NSF) Graduate Research Fellowship Program (GRFP): The NSF GRFP is a fellowship program that awards three years of graduate support, including tuition, stipend, and research allowance, to students pursuing a degree in cybersecurity.

- Minority Science and Engineering Improvement Program (MSEIP): The MSEIP is a program that awards grants to institutions of higher education to support minority students pursuing a degree in cybersecurity.

- National Center for Education Statistics (NCES) Hispanic-Serving Institutions (HSIs) Program: The NCES HSIs Program awards grants to Hispanic-serving institutions to support programs that increase the number of Latino students pursuing a degree in cybersecurity.

- Hispanic College Fund (HCF): The HCF is a non-profit organization that provides scholarships and other financial aid to Latino students pursuing cybersecurity degrees.

- Society of Hispanic Professional Engineers (SHPE) Scholarships: SHPE offers a variety of scholarships to Latino students pursuing a degree in cybersecurity.

- National Society of Black Engineers (NSBE) Scholarships: NSBE offers a variety of scholarships to minority students, including Latino students, pursuing a degree in cybersecurity.

- American Indian Graduate Center (AIGC) Scholarships: AIGC offers a variety of scholarships to Native American students, including Latino students pursuing a degree in cybersecurity.

- Gates Millennium Scholars Program: The Gates Millennium Scholars Program is a scholarship program that awards $20,000 per year for up to eight years to students pursuing a degree in cybersecurity.

- QuestBridge National College Match: QuestBridge is a national college search and scholarship program that matches high-achieving, low-income students with top colleges and universities. Many colleges and universities that participate in QuestBridge offer generous financial aid packages, including scholarships and grants, to students pursuing a degree in cybersecurity.

These are just a few scholarships and financial aid programs available to Latinos interested in cybersecurity. With some research, you should find a program that meets your needs.

Mentorship and internship programs for Latinos in cybersecurity

There are several mentorship and internship programs for Latinos in cybersecurity. Here are a few examples:

- Raíces Cyber Org Mentorship Program: The Raíces Cyber Org Mentorship Program pairs experienced Hispanic and Latinx cybersecurity professionals with mentors to guide and support early-career professionals. The program aims to help mentees develop their skills, knowledge, and networks in the cybersecurity field.

- HITEC Cybersecurity Mentorship Program: The HITEC Cybersecurity Mentorship Program pairs experienced

Hispanic and Latinx cybersecurity professionals with mentors to guide and support early-career professionals. The program aims to help mentees develop their skills, knowledge, and networks in the cybersecurity field.

- LISTA Mentorship Program: The LISTA Mentorship Program pairs experienced Hispanic and Latinx cybersecurity professionals with mentors to guide and support early-career professionals. The program aims to help mentees develop their skills, knowledge, and networks in the cybersecurity field.

- National Hispanic Science Network (NHSN) Cybersecurity Mentorship Program: The NHSN Cybersecurity Mentorship Program pairs experienced Hispanic and Latinx cybersecurity professionals with mentors to guide and support early-career professionals. The program is designed to help mentees develop their skills, knowledge, and networks in the cybersecurity field.

In addition to these programs, there are many other mentorship and internship programs for Latinos in cybersecurity. For example, many cybersecurity companies offer their own mentorship and internship programs. There are also several government-sponsored (CISA, NSA, DoD) mentorship and internship programs for Latinos in cybersecurity.

To find a mentorship or internship program that is right for you, you can start by searching online. Several websites list mentorship and internship programs for Latinos in cybersecurity. You can also contact your local college or university to see if they offer mentorship or internship programs for Latinos in cybersecurity. And don't forget to reach out to the Non-profit organizations listed above, as they have comprehensive lists and opportunities that may not be listed elsewhere.

Here are some suggestions for finding and applying for mentorship and internship programs in cybersecurity:

- **Start your search early.** The best programs are often the most competitive, so starting your search early is essential. This will give you more time to find programs you are eligible for and complete the application process.

- **Be organized.** Keep track of the programs that you apply for and their deadlines. This will help you stay on top of the application process and avoid missing deadlines.

- **Highlight your skills and experience.** When completing your application, be sure to highlight your skills and experience in cybersecurity. This will help you to stand out from other applicants. Sometimes, it's about something different than who has the highest grades, and make sure to sell yourself well.

- **Network with people in the cybersecurity field.** Networking with cybersecurity professionals is a great way to learn about mentorship and internship programs. You can network with people at cybersecurity conferences and events or through social media and professional networking websites.

CHAPTER 6

Your journey has just begun.

Advice for Latinos who are interested in a career in cybersecurity

If you have read this far, it's evident that you possess a curious **mind** and a **genuine interest** in the ever-evolving world of cybersecurity. As you embark on this exciting journey, remember that your path to becoming a successful cybersecurity professional is built with dedication, perseverance, and an unwavering commitment to learning and growth. Here are some points to keep in mind as you continue this path.

First, **get to know other Latinos in the field**. There are many non-profit and professional organizations and communities out there for us. Joining one is a great way to meet new people, learn about new opportunities, and get advice from folks already where you want to be.

Second, **find a mentor**. A mentor can be a valuable guide and support system as you develop your skills and knowledge. You can find a mentor through a professional organization, a school program, or even your network. If you can't find a mentor, join an organization like Raices Cyber Org, where you have a community that can help and guide you as you progress.

Third, **get certified**. Several cybersecurity certifications can help you stand out from other applicants and show potential employers you're serious about your career. Some popular entry-level certifications include the Google Cybersecurity Certificate, ISC2 CC, and Security+.

Fourth, **get experience**. *The best way to learn cybersecurity is by doing it*. There are many ways to gain experience, such as volunteering for cybersecurity projects, working in an IT support role, participating in cybersecurity hackathons & CTFs, and building your home labs and experimenting.

Finally, **stay up-to-date on the latest trends and threats**. The cybersecurity landscape is constantly changing, so staying informed is essential. You can do this by reading cybersecurity blogs and articles, following cybersecurity experts on social media, and attending cybersecurity conferences and events.

Mental Health in Cyber

While technical skills and knowledge are essential for a successful career in cybersecurity, it's equally important to recognize and manage the emotional aspects of the field. Cybersecurity professionals often face complex challenges, high-pressure situations, and the weight of protecting sensitive information. Navigating these emotions and maintaining mental well-being is crucial for long-term success and personal fulfillment.

Never forget to **take care of yourself** as you navigate your career; here are some of the aspects that we ALL need to pay attention to:

Stress and Anxiety: The constant threat of cyberattacks, the urgency of responding to incidents, and the potential for significant consequences can lead to stress and anxiety among cybersecurity professionals. Effective stress management techniques like mindfulness, exercise, and maintaining a healthy work-life balance are essential to cope with these pressures.

Decision Fatigue: Cybersecurity professionals often face a barrage of decisions, each with potential implications for system security and data protection. Decision fatigue can cloud judgment and increase the risk of errors. Prioritization, delegating tasks when possible, and taking regular breaks help alleviate decision fatigue.

Empathy: Cybersecurity is not just about technology; it's about protecting people and understanding their online behavior. Cultivating empathy and understanding human factors can enhance risk assessments, improve communication with non-technical stakeholders, and foster a more resilient security culture.

Continuous Learning and Adaptability: The cybersecurity landscape constantly evolves, and professionals must adapt and embrace lifelong learning. This can lead to feelings of overwhelm or inadequacy. Cultivating a growth mindset, seeking mentorship, and staying up-to-date on emerging trends can help manage these emotions and foster a sense of continuous improvement.

Emotional Resilience and Self-Care: Cybersecurity professionals often face criticism, blame, or threats when responding to security incidents. Emotional resilience and self-care are crucial to maintaining mental health and a positive outlook. Establishing clear boundaries, seeking support from colleagues or mentors, and engaging in activities that promote well-being are essential practices.

In closing, don't forget never stop being passionate about cybersecurity. If you're not passionate about it, it will be tough to succeed in this field. Cybersecurity is challenging but personally rewarding, so being motivated and driven is essential. Be willing to work hard. Cybersecurity is a demanding field, and it can take long hours and hard work to be successful. But if you're passionate about it and willing to work, you can achieve your goals. Be humble. There's always more to learn in cybersecurity. Be humble and open to learning from others.

This guidance will prove helpful as you embark on your cybersecurity journey. Cybersecurity is a thriving and dynamic field brimming with opportunities for growth, development, and making a genuine impact. It's a realm where your skills, knowledge, and passion for technology can converge to safeguard our digital world and protect sensitive information.

Embrace the challenges and complexities that cybersecurity presents. View them not as obstacles but stepping stones to expand your knowledge, refine your skills, and become a seasoned practitioner. Cybersecurity is a dynamic field, constantly evolving, with new threats and technologies emerging every day. Embrace this dynamism, stay abreast of the latest trends, and continuously seek opportunities to enhance your expertise.

Never underestimate the power of networking and collaboration. Surround yourself with like-minded individuals, join communities of cybersecurity professionals, and engage in meaningful discussions and knowledge exchange. Cybersecurity is not a solitary endeavor; it's a collaborative effort where the collective intelligence and experience of the community play a crucial role in safeguarding our digital infrastructure.

As you navigate the cybersecurity landscape, remember that the ultimate goal is to protect our digital infrastructure, safeguard sensitive information, and ensure the security of individuals and organizations. Let this purpose be your guiding light, fueling your passion and driving you toward excellence.

With unwavering determination, a genuine passion for technology, and a commitment to lifelong learning, you have the potential to make a significant impact in the cybersecurity realm. Embrace the challenges, collaborate with your peers, and never let your curiosity fade. The world of cybersecurity eagerly awaits your contributions, eager to benefit from your unique talents and perspectives.

So go get 'em! With your dedication, perseverance, and unwavering commitment to cybersecurity, you'll undoubtedly make a remarkable contribution to this ever-evolving field. Remember, becoming a successful cybersecurity professional is full of challenges. Still, it's also filled with immense rewards, opportunities for growth, and the satisfaction of positively impacting the world.

The future of cybersecurity for Latinos is bright.

There are many reasons for this optimism. First, the demand for cybersecurity professionals is multiplying, and Latinos are well-positioned to meet this demand. Latinos make up a large and growing share of the US population and are increasingly pursuing careers in STEM.

Second, several organizations and initiatives are working to support Latinos in cybersecurity. For example, We at Raices Cyber Org are committed to providing educational, networking, and employment support to cybersecurity professionals from Hispanic, Latino, Latina, and LatinX.

Third, Latinos are bringing unique perspectives and skills to the cybersecurity field. For example, many Latinos are bilingual and bicultural, which can be an asset in working with international clients and partners.

Overall, the future of cybersecurity for Latinos is very bright. With the proper support and resources, Latinos can play a leading role in securing the digital world for everyone.

UNIDOS SE PUEDE / UNITED WE CAN